ATHLETES' FEET

By

The Editors of Runner's World Magazine

Published by

WORLD PUBLICATIONS

World Publications, Box 366, Mountain View, Ca. 94040

CONTENTS

Special Contributing Editor, Steven Subotnick D.P.M., M.S.

Cover Photo by Jay McNally

FOREWORD

"The head cannot say to the feet, 'I have no need for thee.' God has so adjusted the body that there may be no discord. If one member suffers, all suffer together. If one member is honored, all rejoice together."

—I Corinthians

An old gospel song says it a little differently than the Bible: "The foot bone's connected to the ankle bone. The ankle bone's connected to the shin bone. The shin bone's connected..." and so on up the body.

Either way, the message is clear. A person can't say "I feel great except for the pain in my feet." When the feet hurt, he hurts all over, because the feet link up with every other part of the anatomy.

And with athletes, the feet are usually the weakest link in the chain— the one that breaks first. Now that even the postmen are motorized, no one is so dependent on the health of the feet as athletes who run. And, ironically, no one gets their feet hurt as often as athletes.

The foot is built to withstand everyday pounding. But it breaks down when extraordinary stresses are put on it: running in poorly-made, ill-fitting or badly-worn shoes... on hard, smooth surfaces... for too many miles, too fast... with poor running technique... with leg muscles grown tight and out of balance... on legs and feet that heredity has ruled inadequate.

Any one or combination of these factors—shoes, surfaces, overspecialized muscles, form, deformity, overwork—can cause an injury. There are few "accidents" in running. Rarely does a runner step in a hole and turn his ankle. Almost never is he stepped on or kicked by a horse. The things that happen to runners' feet (and are transmitted upward) are nearly always the result of the unusual stresses of running itself.

In a supposedly non-violent sport, the toll is quite high. *Runner's World* polled 1600 of its readers in 1973. One in five of them had suffered knee and achilles tendon injuries severe enough to force a layoff. Almost 10% had shin splints and forefoot problems. Another 7% were stopped by heel, ankle, arch and calf complaints. None of these happened by "accident." All were linked, directly or indirectly, to foot-plant.

In this last fact lies hope. Because most running injuries come from this source, they are predictable and preventable. Threats to foot-leg health can be detected early and dealt with before an injury surfaces. Or if runners get hurt, they can correct the causes instead of accepting temporary, symptomatic relief.

Athletes' Feet is written to help runners read the symptoms and know the causes of their serious foot-related ailments. Notice the word "serious." This doesn't include blisters, fungus infections, ingrown toenails or smelly feet. These are relatively minor complaints.

"Minor complaints aren't complaints to runners," says Dr. Steve Subotnick, a California podiatrist who contributes heavily to this booklet. "They only complain when they can't run properly."

Proper running starts—and often ends—at ground level.

What Happens?

by George Sheehan M.D.

Dr. Sheehan, "Medical Advice" columnist for Runner's World, addressed these remarks to a sports medicine seminar sponsored by the California College of Podiatric Medicine in San Francisco. They are published with the college's permission.

I am a cardiologist, but my relationship to sports medicine has been as an athlete rather than a doctor. What I have experienced as a runner—and what judgment I have been able to bring to this experience as a physician—have convinced me that traditional medicine isn't dealing adequately with athletic problems.

In more than 10 years as a distance runner, I have experienced almost every injury of the foot, leg, knee, thigh and back. During that time, the medical profession has only been able to provide me with symptomatic relief. It wasn't until I came under the care of a podiatrist (foot specialist) that I was able to run for prolonged periods and be free of foot, leg and knee difficulties. The podiatrist treated me by restoring the structural balance of my feet.

Yet the medical profession has been slow in adopting this method of treatment which obviously is effective. The standard treatment of the most common ailment of runners, chondromalacia of the knee (which I call "runner's knee" because the technical term is so clumsy) is a case in point. Runner-patients are still advised to rest, wear casts, try a variety of medications, do quadriceps exercises and, when all else fails, to undergo surgery.

In my first years as medical columnist for *Runner's World*, I made these same suggestions to the victims of runner's knee. There must, you see, be a standard operating procedure—even if it doesn't work.

Meanwhile, I was getting hints that the foot was the cause of it all. A high school runner told me that he had trouble with his knee if he wore a certain pair of shoes. Another runner had pain while using a banked track. I had knee pain and found it was due to the slant of the road. My left knee gave me trouble if I ran with traffic. I cured the pain by running against traffic, and thought no more of it.

No more, that is, until I began a lengthy correspondence with Tom Bache, an ex-Marine and a fine runner in the San Diego area. Tom had suffered from runner's knee for two years when we began to exchange ideas. He had gone through every therapy suggested in the literature (short of surgery), without success. As soon as he got back to running, the pain returned.

I wrote to Tom about the crown-of-the-road idea and about running on the outside of the foot. This helped him until he would forget, get tired or lose form in a race. So his problem continued. Neither Tom nor I thought of the next logical step, foot supports, until his arch started to bother him and he sought help from runner-podiatrist Dr. John Pagliano

Dr. Pagliano fitted Bache for supports, and *voila!* Tom lost his knee pain and in a matter of weeks was up to marathon training. He ran the best marathon of his career shortly thereafter.

After this experience, I saw the number one man on a local college cross-country team. He had symptoms of severe runner's knee. I looked at his feet, and even to a cardiologist his problems seemed evident. His feet were a disaster area. After podiatric treatment, he returned to running again within a week and was completely asymptomatic.

Soon I was seeing tennis players with the same problem, and hearing about more and more runners who were being helped with drug store supports, and others who had reached to podiatrists for treatment and were back to full-scale running. The treatment was successful not only for knee pain but for the gamut of injuries along the foot-leg chain.

This convinced me that no matter what an athlete's complaint is, we should look first to his feet as the source of the trouble. The foot is an architectural marvel—an engineering masterpiece which has 26 bones, four times as many ligaments, and an intricate network of tendons which act as guy-ropes or slings for the arches. When these components are perfectly balanced, the foot can handle almost any amount of work. However, even a minute deviation from normal can cause adjustments that will eventually produce injury either in the foot, or in its supporting muscles and tendons, or even in the structures above it.

When this happens, we have familiar afflictions such as heel spurs, achilles tendinitis, shin splints, calf pulls, stress fractures and the ubiquitous runner's knee. In sports medicine, these problems are lumped under the category of "overuse syndromes." It was originally felt that excess activity was the sole cause of the trouble, and remedies were directed to relieving discomfort, to allowing a suitable period of rest and then to resuming the training activity.

Unfortunately, the presence of an "X" factor was not suspected and therefore was left uncorrected. Hence, the result of therapy was predictable. The athlete went through a sequence of pain, followed by relief through rest and treatment, and then a return of pain when training was resumed.

The long-suffering athletes cried, "Why me? Why a good guy like me? Why should I have trouble with my feet (or legs or knees) when my teammates who practice as much as I do have no difficulty?"

The answer is that the ailing athlete has an inherent susceptibility to his injury. And this susceptibility, the "X" factor which the medical profession is so slow to recognize, was a structurally weak foot.

THE NORMAL FOOT

What's normal in a foot? The semantics are confusing here, because "normal" could be "odd," and "average" could be "abnormal."

Dr. George Sheehan, a heart man who has been made an honorary foot doctor by the American Podiatry Association for his service to that specialty, writes that even the healthiest feet are a bit weird:

"The feet—those odd-looking structures—may be a scientific triumph, but certainly aren't an artistic one. Chesterton once wrote that anyone who could look at his feet without laughing must be devoid of a sense of humor."

Feet aren't pretty, perhaps, but they're functional—most of the time. *Some* of the time? Podiatrists who treat feet as a profession indicate that a minority of feet are without structural or functional flaws.

"The normal foot is one which, during function, places no undue stress upon itself, or on the joints of the ankle, knee or hip," says Dr. Steve Subotnick, executive secretary of the American Academy of Podiatric Sports Medicine. " 'Normal' does not mean 'average,' since the average foot function for a given population may be abnormal."

More likely than not, according to Dr. Subotnick, the average athlete

VIEWS OF A NORMAL FOOT

Heel and lower leg are perpendicular to ground; forefoot is parallel with ground when heel is perpendicular.

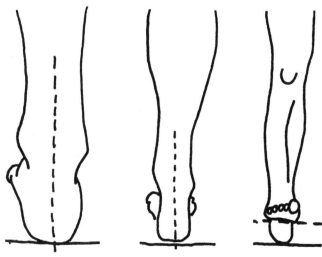

Anatomy of the Foot

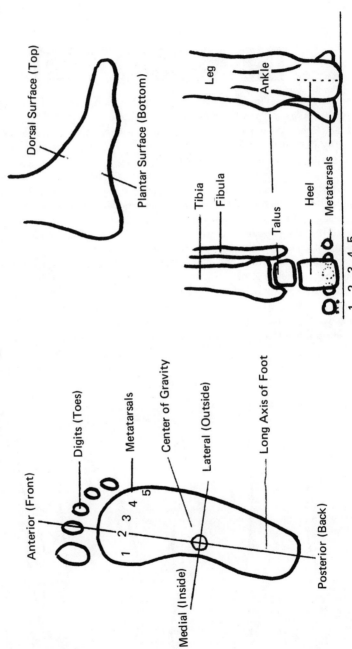

Dorsal Surface (Top)

Plantar Surface (Bottom)

Leg

Ankle

Tibia

Fibula

Talus

Heel

Metatarsals

1 2 3 4 5

Anterior (Front)

Digits (Toes)

Metatarsals

Center of Gravity

Lateral (Outside)

Long Axis of Foot

Medial (Inside)

Posterior (Back)

1 2 3 4 5

has an abnormality. And the stress of sport is almost certain to uncover it. These abnormalities are a prime suspect in the injuries that disable two in every three runners during their careers.

Before runners can know what's wrong with their feet and what to do about it, they need to define what's right and normal in their function. Basically, the foot has two roles:

1. *Acting as a flexible shock-absorber on landing.*

2. *Acting as a rigid lever during push-off.*

Steve Subotnick explains, "A normal foot is one which, at heel strike, allows for accommodation on uneven surfaces. Normally, about four degrees of motion will take place at the heel during contact. Following the heel contact, the foot becomes more rigid until at toe-off it functions as a rigid lever."

The doctor wrote in an earlier booklet, *Shoes for Runners*, "I consider a normal foot as one with the heel perpendicular to the ground when the runner is standing on both feet. The leg is roughly perpendicular to the floor. The metatarsal heads (bones at the base of the toes) are on the floor when the heel is perpendicular. In this way, a plumbline dropped from the hip joint would fall through the thigh, through the lower leg, and come out just a little inside of the heel." (See page 7.)

Without this lineup, the feet don't function as they should. They don't give the proper shock absorption or leverage. The "undue stresses" Dr. Subotnick mentioned are put on the foot and related structures.

Nature short-changed a large percentage of us in the area of foot construction, and tampering with nature's surfaces has compounded the problem.

Dr. Subotnick: "Man's foot was meant to function on uneven surfaces such as those present in fields, meadows, sandy beaches or jungle floors. The invention of man-made surfaces such as concrete and asphalt places extreme stress upon the foot, which wasn't meant to accept it. Because of this, it is estimated that 90% of the population will at some time have a foot complaint."

THE ABNORMAL FOOT

by Steven Subotnick D.P.M.

Dr. Subotnick, associate professor of biomechanics and surgery at the California College of Podiatric Medicine, practices in Hayward, Calif. He is an experienced long distance runner with several marathons to his credit.

If the normal foot has its forefoot flat on the floor, lower leg in line with the heel bone and the heel perpendicular to the surface, then obviously the abnormal foot is one in which these relationships don't exist. Yet the foot continues to seek its "normal" position as it functions. And the resulting twist-

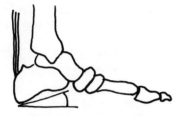

NORMAL ARCH. Heel bone at proper angle (note small tip on top of that bone, in front of achilles tendon; this is normal).

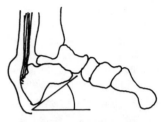

"CAVUS" (HIGH-ARCHED) FOOT. Greater than normal pitch of heel bone, causing tip to rub on tissue and irritate the tissues.

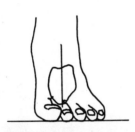

NORMAL FOOT PLANT. (left foot). Line drawn through heel bone is per-perpendicular to ground and parallel to bisection of the lower one-third of leg.

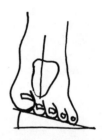

FOREFOOT VARUS (left foot). Heel bone is normal, but forefoot has a pronounced out-wart tilt, resulting in an irritating roll of the foot as it compensates.

ing, turning and compensating puts unusual strains on the foot and leg—strains which predispose athletes to injuries.

Here is a simplified guide to the most common abnormalities. They often occur in various combinations, and there are others which aren't described here. While athletes are not advised to diagnose and treat all of their own problems, they can profit by knowing the sources of their trouble.

Toes—"Morton's Foot" is Dr. George Sheehan's pet topic. He has written of it often in *Runner's World*. Basically, this is a deformity characterized by (1) a short big toe and a longer second toe; (2) a hypermobile first metatarsal, and (3) misplacement of the small sesamoid bones under the metatarsal heads. This combination causes faulty weight-bearing in the foot.

Although this problem is more common than generally recognized, few doctors yet consider it significant. Dr. Sheehan, however, is convinced it is a leading cause of runners' complaints.

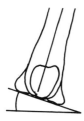 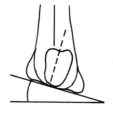

TIBIAL VARUM
(right foot). Entire
lower leg is out of line.
Landing is on the out-
side of the foot, with
a twisting motion need-
ed to meet the ground.

SUBTALAR VARUS
(right foot). Heel bone
is out of alignment with
the rest of the lower
leg, resulting in improp-
er foot plant and a
compensating roll.

Sheehan has written in *RW*, "Morton's Foot (visible) occurs in about 33% of the general population. However, in a patient population of 1000 studied by Dr. Richard Schuster, 80% of the patients had the short first toe/ long second configuration. No x-ray studies were done to determine how many of the other 20% had occult forms of Morton's Foot. Probably all of them."

Dr. Sheehan feels Morton's Foot is responsible for, among other ailments, a great number of stress fractures in the small bones of the foot. He writes, "I recently surveyed all the available x-rays and orthopedic texts in the local hospital and discovered that *every* stress fracture pictured in these books had occurred in a Morton's Foot!"

Forefoot—Normally, when the heel is in a neutral position (about per-pendicular), the entire forefoot rests on the ground. But frequently, the neu-tral heel is accompanied by the first and second metatarsal heads failing to touch the ground. We call this deformity "forefoot varus." If the outer me-tatarsal heads are raised, the technical name is "forefoot *valgus.*"

In order for the "varus" forefoot to contact the ground, the heel must turn in. This is abnormal. When the forefoot varus deformity approaches four degrees, it becomes mildly symptomatic. Beyond this amount, the symptoms can become severe, particularly when accentuated by the stress of running.

Individuals with this deformity are prone to postural fatigue as their muscles work overtime to support the foot. They complain of pain in the backs of their legs and in their arches, and are more comfortable pacing the floor than standing in one place. The turning in of the foot to accommodate the fore-foot varus also causes internal rotation of the leg. This may result in knee, hip or low-back pain.

Arch—Dr. Gabe Mirkin writes in *The Complete Runner*, "The name 'flat foot' implies that the longitudinal arch is flat. This is virtually never the case. The entire foot is rolled inward and gives the appearance that the arch is flat. Cup your hand and place it on the table. Now roll the hand inward. The 'arch' will seem to disappear. This is what happens with 'flat feet.' "

A seemingly flat arch is a symptom that a deformity is present somewhere in the foot-leg structure. This causes the foot to rotate inward, to pronate, to an excessive degree on foot contact. Pronation, a leading contributor to injuries, can come from any of several of the deformities listed here.

However, an excessively high arch isn't such a good type to have, either. It may appear to be high because the heel contacts on the outer border. This, too, can lead to injury complications.

Ankle–During running, the foot has to flex upward about 10 degrees. The ankle must have enough flexibility for this to happen. If this motion is impeded, the foot collapses to compensate.

Two muscles in the back of the leg, the gastrocnemius and soleus, are attached to the achilles tendon, which in turn inserts into the heel bone. When either of the muscles is tight and the leg bone can't easily move the required 10 degrees over the foot, an unusual strain is placed on the achilles tendon and the shin area. We call this lack of flexibility an "equinus" deformity.

Knee–This isn't simply a knee problem, but the use of the knee as a reference point simplifies the description of two deformities: "knock-kneed" and "bow-legged."

Individuals who are knock-kneed have what podiatrists call "tibial valgum." The knees rub together while the heels are wide apart. This places abnormal stress upon the inside of the foot, and tends to prolong or accentuate the pronation (turning in of the foot) at heel strike. The foot never becomes a rigid lever for propulsion of the forefoot, and therefore is subjected to abnormal stresses. This failure to stabilize the foot can lead to the formation of bunions.

In the bow-legged deformity– "tibial *varum*"–the knees are far apart when the feet are together. The heel strikes the ground at an angle and must pronate to function properly. At heel strike, there normally is about four degrees of pronation. But bow-legged people exceed this amount. The result: pains in both the foot and knee–most commonly, runner's knee or heel bumps.

Leg–Limb-length discrepancies (one leg slightly shorter than the other) can be a disabling problem to runners. Although major differences are usually recognized at a young age, the more minor ones often go unnoticed until symptoms develop, ranging from low-back pain to sciatica. Sciatica is an irritation of the nerve running the length of the leg, and is one of the most persistent and frustrating ailments a runner can have.

There are two types of limb-length discrepancies. The first is anatomical, in which there is actual shortening of one limb, causing a tilt of the pelvis and compensation along the spinal column.

The second type is termed "functional." It develops from abnormal positioning of the hip and subsequent spasm of muscles, or abnormal positioning of one foot with a pelvic rotation.

Limb-length discrepancies as small as one-quarter of an inch can produce symptoms in runners. In fact, in all the deformities described here, variations of fractions of inches from normal are extremely significant.

CAUSE AND EFFECT

Lots of things happen to runners when their feet are abnormal, and most of what happens is bad. Some runners escape with nagging little aches and pains that drain away their interest in the sport and prevent them from reaching the levels they want. Too many of them are stopped, temporarily or permanently, by injuries.

The casualty figures are high. If we think of a "serious" injury as one requiring a layoff from running, a doctor's care or both, then the odds are 2-1 that a runner will be seriously hurt. More depressing yet is the fact that these injuries tend to occur in combinations (a sore arch and a sore knee at the same time, for instance), and they repeat themselves when the causes are left untreated.

Here are some statistics. They're based on independent surveys of injured runners, one by *Runner's World* and another by Dr. Richard Schuster of New York City, a podiatrist with a large athletic clientele. *RW* questioned about 1600 runners. Dr. Schuster randomly selected 100 cases from his files of runner-patients.

The figures (combined from the two studies, which have almost identical rankings and percentages) show the incidence of injury to 10 different areas of the feet and legs. Within each general area, there are several possibilities for problems. We'll talk about them momentarily.

1.	Knee	24.8%	6.	Arch	8.1%
2.	Achilles Tendon	17.5%	7.	Heel	7.8%
3.	Forefoot	10.4%	8.	Hamstring	5.4%
4.	Shin	10.3%	9.	Hip	3.5%
5.	Ankle	8.8%	10.	Calf	3.4%

KNEE

Knee pains make up one-quarter of the total number of injuries. But as many as three-quarters of the injured runners have it, Dr. Schuster reports. Although they may be in to see him for another ailment, the sore knee is a common—almost universal—complaint.

It's so prevalent that the pain under the kneecap known technically as "chondromalacia" is generally referred to as "runner's knee." Dr. George Sheehan calls this the "Dutch Elm Disease of long distance runners."

Chondromalacia, an irritation of the cartilage on the underside of the kneecap, occurs when the kneecap fails to glide properly along the groove of the femur bone. The most common cause, according to podiatrists, is abnormal pronation (turning in or flattening of the feet) on contact with the ground. Pronation results from a number of different deformities.

Dr. Steve Subotnick details the case of a runner:

"He related that his knees were so painful that he could not run any more. The pain was under the kneecap and there was a grating sensation whenever he would walk up and down stairs or sat for awhile and then tried to stand up.

"Examination of his feet showed that he had a moderate amount of instability that would probably cause no problems for everyday walking, but was significant in long distance running. He compensated for his deformity by pronating, or flattening his feet. As he pronated, his legs internally rotated and his kneecaps went towards the outside of the knee, causing a grating and painful sensation."

Dr. Subotnick fitted his patient with custom-made inserts for his shoes and prescribed strengthening-stretching exercises. The runner who had been struggling with 3½ hours in the marathon soon was breaking three hours consistently. In the two years since he was treated, there had been no recurrence of knee pain.

ACHILLES TENDON

A longtime runner had been limping along on painful achilles tendons for almost 10 years when three podiatrists told him why he hurt this way.

The first said it had to do with exercise, and the lack of it: "Your calves are unusually strong and tight, even for a runner. You're overdeveloped there from your years of running. Your achilles tendon is like a rubber band that is

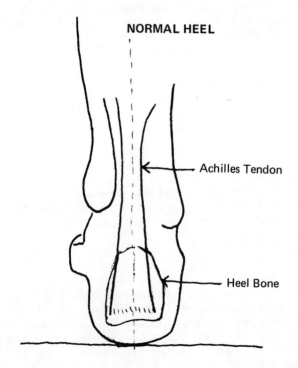

NORMAL HEEL

Achilles Tendon

Heel Bone

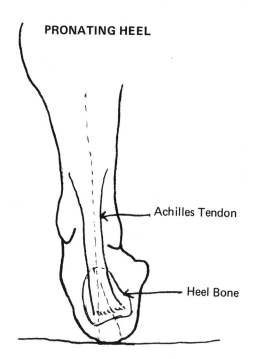

PRONATING HEEL

Achilles Tendon

Heel Bone

always stretched to the point of breaking. When you put the slightest extra pull on it, something gives."

The achilles tendon is a cord connecting the powerful calf muscles to the heel bone. At its narrowest point, just above the heel, it's no bigger around than a finger. An overstressed tendon usually "gives" at this point.

Inflexibility is one reason why this happens. Another is an excessive twisting of the heel bone, the "calcaneus." The long-suffering runner had this explained to him in writing by Dr. John Pagliano, who said, "Various foot disorders—some mild, some severe—can cause a rotation of the calcaneus. Since the achilles tendon is attached to the back of the calcaneus, it becomes stretched beyond its normal length."

When inflexibility combines with this deformity, achilles tendon pain often develops. There are degrees to achilles problems. The most common and least severe is "tendinitis," an inflammation of the tendon. The second degree is "partial rupture," in which tendon fibers are torn. The third degree is "complete rupture," a total break in the tendon.

A third podiatrist told the achilles-sore runner that he had a "tibial varum" deformity, a bow-legged style of running that caused him to pronate excessively at foot plant.

With inserts for his shoes and stretching exercises for his legs, the runner brought his achilles tendon problem under control. The damage of 10 years would leave him permanently vulnerable in this area, but most of his running was now pain-free.

FOREFOOT

If we're to believe Dr. Dudley Morton and his latter-day supporter Dr. George Sheehan, every forefoot problem springs from improper weight-bearing by the small metatarsal bones. "Morton's Foot," this deformity is called. Its most obvious sign is a second toe longer than the first.

As Dr. Sheehan mentioned in the previous chapter, *every* stress fracture of the metatarsals which he saw on x-rays and in medical literature occurred on a Morton's Foot.

"In addition," Sheehan writes, "every Morton's Foot I could find in these books showed an enlarged and widened second metatarsal. This is proof that the weight distribution is abnormal."

Podiatrist Richard Schuster adds, "Most runners with metatarsal problems have either a short first metatarsal (Morton's Syndrome) and/or a varus forefoot (the inner forefoot is off the ground when the heel is perpendicular to the surface). While Morton's Syndrome has been played down in the management of foot problems, it appears to be a very significant factor in foot complaints among runners."

Dr. Steve Subotnick notes that treatment is not difficult. "One simply must place a build-up under the first metatarsal head and have no corresponding buildup under the second metatarsal head. This can be done simply by using eighth-inch felt." (See page 38.)

SHIN

Stress fractures occur in the long bone down the front of the leg as well as in the feet. And what athletes call "shin splints" may indeed be a tiny bone crack. Whatever the cause, a break or the true shin splint (inflammation of the tissues surrounding the bone), the pain may be equally devastating to a runner.

Dr. Richard Schuster thinks the major culprit in shin splints is muscular imbalance. The muscles which pull ("dorsiflex") the foot are weak. The opposing muscles in the calf are short and tight, and don't let the foot flex to its normal 10 degrees. The shins get hurt in this struggle.

Schuster says, "Shin splints occur almost exclusively among runners with short calf muscles. Treatment is directed primarily at the calf muscle. This includes calf stretching exercises and the use of inserts with long heel lifts.

William F. Leach, of the University of Illinois/Chicago Circle, suggests another possible cause of shin splints. He did film studies comparing shin splints sufferers with non-sufferers. The healthy runners' feet and legs were 2-5 degrees "straighter" (closer to perpendicular) on landing than the sore-shinned legs. Leach said this slight difference in angle "over an extended period of time could possibly result in musculo-tendinous strain."

ANKLE

The ranking of ankle ailments probably is higher than it should be. Nearly all the ankle injuries that do show up in runners are the result of accidents, bad shoes or running on out-of-shape feet and legs. Deformities account for few problems in this area.

Ankle sprains are easily explained away. (They're not so easily dealt with.) The cause is usually nothing more exotic than a misstep on rough ground.

Pain that shows up on the outside tendon of the ankle is frequently caused by inadequate or badly-worn shoes. The heel is too narrow, therefore unstable. Or it's too mushy; it compacts and rolls to the outside on contact. Or the heel has ground down from wear, exaggerating the tendency to run on the outer edge of the foot.

Beginning runners, women especially, seem prone to strains, swelling and tenderness around the ankles. Writing in the booklet *The Female Runner*, Dr. Joan Ullyot says, "The most common single injury (among beginner women) seems to be stress-induced tendinitis on the outside of the foot and ankle. However, there is no history of a sudden wrench. The swelling just appears."

Fitness, shoes with stable heels and watching one's step will take care of most ankle complaints.

ARCH AND HEEL

Since the worst arch problem among runners comes at the point where the arch and heel meet, we can talk of arch and heel injuries together.

A fibrous band called the "plantar fascia" connects the ball of the foot with the heel. It attaches to the bottom of the heel at the back of the arch. And it is here that deep, stubborn pain develops. It feels at first like a bruise, and is usually ignored until the runner can't run on it any more. Inflamma-

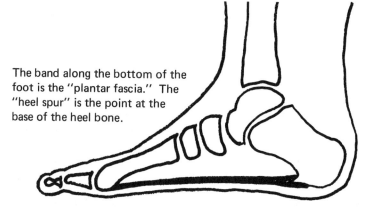

The band along the bottom of the foot is the "plantar fascia." The "heel spur" is the point at the base of the heel bone.

tion sets in, then a calcium deposit may form at this spot. The runner has what's known as "heel spur syndrome." If ignored too long, the "spur" may have to be removed surgically.

A marathoner, one of the best in the country in the late 1960s, developed a severe pain at that spot. He had the surgery, and still didn't get much relief. At times, he couldn't run a hundred steps without pain. He saw many doctors and tried many different types of inserts. Only after being treated by a podiatrist Steve Subotnick did he get back to marathon distances. Five of the runner's potentially best years had passed in the meantime.

Several runner-podiatrists agree that this type of plantar fascia strain is common to runners with an excessively high-arched foot. A related heel ailment also has a special attraction to runners with high arches (among other deformities which cause heel rotation). This is the bump on the top and back of the heel.

Dr. Subotnick explains, "The movement of the heel bone causes irritation of the tissue overlying the achilles tendon as it passes over the calcaneus (heel bone). Initially, there is blistering of the skin. In time, a bump begins to form between the shin and the tendon, and the tendon and the bone. The bump is partly an enlarged, inflamed bursa (fluid-filled protective sac) and partly a calcium deposit."

The bony growth may begin to cut away at the tendon like a hack-saw. If this happens, the deposit has to be removed surgically. It won't go away by itself. But while the doctor is cutting, he also has to be thinking how he'll remove the *cause* of the trouble. Otherwise, another bump may form.

HAMSTRING AND HIP

Pulled hamstrings are a sprinter's ailment, and come from sources other than the feet. Persistent soreness in the backs of the legs and in the hips, however, afflicts all runners and is often foot-related.

Pains through the hips and buttocks and down the backs of the legs are frequently symptoms of sciatica. Dr. George Sheehan calls the sciatic nerve "the longest river of pain in the body." It originates in the lower back and travels to the toes, and gives off pain, numbness or a tingling sensation when it's irritated.

One source of irritation is a difference in leg lengths. Dr. Steve Subotnick describes one such case:

"A college distance runner (who had competed in the 1972 Olympic Trials) came to my office complaining of extreme shooting-type pains that radiated from his back down one leg. For the previous six months, running had been almost impossible and he was becoming stiff to the point where he could just barely stretch his hands beyond his knees when bending over.

"The young runner had sought the advice of several medical specialists, whose opinions ranged from back strain to disc herniation. One specialist suggested back surgery as possible aid."

Subotnick discovered that the runner had one foot that was nearly flat, the other with a high arch, and the pelvis was lower on the side with the flattened foot. With support for the flat arch, the pelvic tilt was corrected and the sciatic pain soon disappeared. The athlete ran better times than ever before.

CALF

Dr. Richard Schuster sees hundreds of athletes, and notices that with few exceptions they're tight in the calves. He writes, "The act of running tends to tighten the calf muscles. Most runners are unable to dorsiflex (pull up) the foot to the ideal 10 degrees beyond the right angle. Many runners, especially the 'hobby' runners, tend to neglect warmups and stretching exercises."

They get hurt in the calves for much the same reasons they get achilles tendon and shin problems: muscle inflexibility, which compounds basic foot-leg deformities.

Self-Help

"When you hear hoofbeats, think of horses—not zebras."

Podiatrist Steve Subotnick used this line to end an article about athletic injuries. His point was, "Look first for the obvious, the common, the simple explanation of why you're hurting. Don't forget that and look for something more exotic."

Most ways that runners get hurt are obvious to even a slightly trained eye. The most common injuries are rather simple to diagnose and treat. That is, if you have some idea what to look for, and you find it before too much damage is done.

We're not trying to train amateur doctors with this booklet, only first-aid personnel. Just as you sometimes have to take your car into the shop for major overhauls, you also have to take yourself into the doctor's office for the big repair jobs. But you save the doctor's time and your money by doing the everyday preventive maintenance on yourself.

It doesn't take a professional to spot the most obvious problems. And it doesn't take any special training or tools to fix them. Any runner can practice do-it-yourself podiatry if he can link up the causes and effects outlined in the first chapter.

"Most of the complaints," writes Dr. Richard Schuster, "appear to be partially or completely related to (1) structural shortcomings of the foot; (2) the manner in which the foot functions, or (3) the environment in which the foot functions—footwear and running surfaces. It therefore follows that the most complaints may be helped by treating the feet."

But you first have to know what it is you're treating. This series of questions and comments will help you in your detective work. They relate to the general areas of the ailment's history and symptoms, your basic foot-leg anatomy, footwear and methods of treatment.

How did it happen?

Did the pain come on suddenly or gradually? Did it first make itself felt during running or later? A characteristic of the stress-related injuries of sports

is that they don't hurt too much right away. An achilles tendon sufferer tells
what happened to him:

"I ran hard one-lappers in spikes on the tight turns of an indoor track.
There was no 'snapping.' I didn't grab my leg and hobble to a stop, scream-
ing, 'I'm hurt!' I just felt a little twinge in my right leg. I finished the workout and thought nothing more of the pain until the next morning. When I
stepped out of bed, I fell down. The tendon was so sore and swollen I couldn't
walk."

Only after the runner had slept on his injury did he notice it. He had a
typical delayed-reaction pain. Many running pains come on even more subtly.
They start small and sneak up on you over a period of days or weeks—so slowly you can't pin a date or circumstances on their origin.

Be alert for signs of the smallest pain, because knowing how it started
is an important first step in finding out how to treat it.

When did it happen?

The life-span of soreness is a clue to its seriousness. How long have you
been hurting—a day, a week, a month? A runner is as sure to get sore as a
swimmer is to get wet. But there are normal pains and abnormal ones, and you
need to know the difference.

Muscle soreness after an unaccustomed bout of exercise is normal and
fleeting. A post-race "hangover" is an example. You're stiff the morning after, perhaps stiffer still the day after that. But all traces of pain should be gone
in three or four days to a week. Simply moderate activity until they disappear.

The serious ones are those which hang on for a week or more—feeling the
same as before or getting worse. You know you're injured when you've hurt
this long, when there's a redness and/or swelling in the sore area, or when it
doesn't "loosen up" as you run.

What were you doing?

You get hurt by doing the things you're not used to doing. That should
be obvious. But athletes continue to make sudden changes in their routines.
The 10 most dangerous leaps are the ones from:

1. Inactivity to full activity.
2. Low- to high-mileage training.
3. Slow to fast training.
4. Flat running to hill running.
5. Grass and dirt running to road running.
6. Roads to the track.
7. Flat shoes to spiked shoes.
8. Well-heeled to unheeled shoes.
9. Well-supported to flimsy shoes.
10. Old to new shoes or vice versa.

The human body has amazing adaptive potential. But athletes must
meet it halfway by allowing an appropriate break-in period.

Have you run on it?

Dr. Steve Subotnick has said a "serious" injury to a runner is one he can't run through. Anything less is mere inconvenience. There are degrees of seriousness, and runners usually are too impatient to deal with them as nature's healing processes dictate.

First degree: By enduring some pain, the runner can continue his normal routine. He ignores his symptoms and the pain often graduates to higher degrees.

Second degree: He can still run, but only in a limited way—no hills, nothing fast, nothing too long. He runs, favoring the injured part and inviting sympathetic pains.

Third degree: Can't run, but can walk or bicycle and does so with abandon.

Fourth degree: Total immobilization. Craving activity, any activity, and jumping back into it before he's ready.

John "Jock" Semple—a physiotherapist between Boston marathons—says injured runners are like impatient farmers who pull up their carrots to see if they're growing. "Once you pull them up," says Semple, "you can't put them back in the ground again. As soon as (runners) can get back on their feet, they're trying to run hard again—to see if they're okay."

Has this happened before?

An ex-runner tells of having calcium deposits cut out of his heels twice and needing a third operation when he gave up the sport in disgust. That's what happens when causes of injuries aren't treated along with the symptoms. The potential for future trouble remains.

Were you hurt this way before? Remember how it happened. Were the circumstances similar? Were the pains the same? What did you do to treat them? More importantly, what did you leave uncorrected that might explain this re-run of an old problem?

Repeated episodes of injury are almost certain evidence of basic mechanical problems in the feet and legs.

Where does it hurt?

Strange as this may sound, you probably won't be centering treatment on the sore spot. The *source* of trouble is likely to be somewhere else.

Remember Dr. George Sheehan's discussion of knee injuries in Chapter One? He told how Tom Bache suffered through "every therapy in the literature (short of surgery) without success." Then Tom developed arch pain and visited a podiatrist for that. When the arch was supported, the knee trouble disappeared.

No matter where you hurt—knee, calf, achilles, shin—consider the feet guilty until they're proven innocent.

Can you run on it?

Does it hurt most when you're running or not running? Does it feel worst when you first get up in the morning, then gradually better as you warm up, or the other way around? In general, the most serious injuries are the ones that hurt more and more during a run. The ones that feel better as you loosen up aren't so severe.

Notice how pains respond to exercise. Run very cautiously, say for 5-10 minutes. If the pain worsens, you'll know it by then. Stop! If you're feeling almost normal, you're probably safe in going on for a while.

Watch, too, how your injury reacts to different kinds of running—fast vs. slow, continuous vs. interrupted, short vs. long, soft vs. hard surfaces, hills vs. flats—and different kinds of footwear. Then choose the ones, if any, which don't aggravate it.

How long is your second toe?

Is it longer than the big toe? If it is, you have the most obvious type of Morton's Foot. The foot doesn't support your weight as it should. Among many other problems, you're highly susceptible to stress fractures in the small bones of the forefoot.

Do your heels have bumps?

Bumps, usually accompanied by redness and tenderness, form where the achilles tendon inserts into the heel bone at the back of the foot. They signal any of several mechanical irregularities in the foot—the most common being an extra-high arch and a bow-legged style of running. These deformities spawn injuries both in the heel itself and in areas distant from it.

What shape are your feet in?

Is the arch high or flat? Is the forefoot narrow or wide? Dr. Gabe Mirkin writes in *The Complete Runner*, "A review of chronic leg injuries in runners during one year revealed that 82% had an 'inverted' (commonly called 'flat') foot, and 60% had a 'B' or narrower width yet were not wearing narrow shoes. More than half of the injuries were in runners with *both* an inverted foot and a shoe that did not fit."

How do your knees line up?

Stand up with the heels and knees together. Can you do it without straining? If the knees are together yet the heels don't touch, you have "tibial valgum." That simply means you're knock-kneed, and according to Dr. Steve Subotnick, "This places abnormal stress upon the inside of the foot," tending to flatten it. Bunions are one result.

If the heels touch but the knees don't, the deformity is called "tibial varum." You're bow-legged. Dr. Subotnick noted in Chapter One that this causes the heel to strike at an exaggerated angle and twsit inward to an excessive degree. Heel bumps may develop.

How level is your pelvis?

The pelvic crests are the sharp bones above the hips. If you're a normally skinny runner, they're quite prominent. Stand relaxed and straight before a mirror, and poke your index fingers into the flesh at the top of these bones. Are the fingers level or is one noticeably lower than the other? If it is, look down at the arches. The one on the low side may be flatter than the other. These are signs of a leg-length difference which may produce sciatica or hip pain.

How flexible are you?

As long as you're standing anyway, keep the legs straight and bend forward. Can you put your fingertips to the floor without straining? Many runners can't because the muscles in the backs of their legs are too tight. Tight calves, which in turn lead to inflexibility at the ankle, breed injuries ranging from achilles tendinitis to shin splints.

What shoes do you use?

Dr. Richard Schuster, who has tested as many injured runners as any podiatrist in the US, states flatly, "Much of the foot gear worn by runners appears to be made with little concern for the functional needs of runners." To meet those functional needs, a distance running flat should have these features:

1. Adequate heel height—a "lift" to take strain off the back of the legs; as high or higher than your street shoes.

2. Adequate heel width— to reduce instability or "roll" on impact; as wide or wider than the upper.

3. Adequate heel support—a rigid "counter" around the back of the upper to further stabilize the heel.

4. Stiff, solid "shank"—no cutout space under the arch; a shoe that is flat and rigid from heel to ball.

5. Flexible forefoot—allowing plenty of bend from the ball of the foot forward; you should be able to bend the shoe double upfront.

A weakness in any of these areas can cause an injury or slow its healing.

How do the shoes fit?

Dick Buerkle, a US national champion on the track, had a long history of shin splints. Then a hurdler friend told him that slippage—both on the ground and inside his too-big shoes—was to blame.

"So I got a snug-fitting pair of shoes," Buerkle says, "and I ran on the roads—because you can't slip on concrete. The shin splints went away."

The heel, too, should be snug-fitting. Dr. Gabe Mirkin points out, "A heel that fits loosely into the shoe will wobble with each plant and put undue strain on the achilles."

How are the shoes wearing?

Running in a worn out shoe is an invitation to injury. But watching the *way* the shoe wears is a clue to preventing those injuries.

Dr. Steve Subotnick writes in *Shoes for Runners*, "A normal foot will show normal wear. Typically, there is more extensive wear on the outside of the heel than on the inside, but not so excessive that the shoes are totally worn out on the outer heel within a few weeks—before the rest of the shoe shows significant wear.

"Wear should progress on the outside of the shoe, underneath the ball of the foot at the level of the first metatarsal head, then out through the great toe."

It's normal for peak wear to occur just outside of center at the rear of the heel. However, Subotnick says, "If the runner has excessive bowing of the legs, there will be extensive wearing on the outside of the heel—farther out than normal. If the individual tends to flatten out or pronate the foot, there will be more wear at the back of the heel—or even on the inside edge."

What have you done for the injury?

Injured runners will try anything. Bob Carman wrote of his heel trouble in *Guide to Distance Running*:

"I have been soaked (hot and cold), infra-redded and ultra-violated; taped and strapped; fed salt, vitamins A, B (1 through 12), C, D, E and K, wheat germ oil, cod liver oil, castor oil; had heels added inside and outside my shoes; changed running surfaces from grass to road to sand to track to grass, and so on; tried fartlek, interval training, LSD, SSD and even LFD; gave up sex, tried hourly sex; had cortisone shots to the point where one massive dose knocked me unconscious; have been plied with various medicines from aspirin to muscle relaxants to anti-inflammatory enzymes (and probably inflammatory enzymes if there are any); taken pills of all persuasions from thyroidal to hemorrhoidal; been vibrated with ultra-sound, x-rays, ice massage and galvanic shock. I have even tried—God forbid—rest. All to no avail."

None of this seemed to get to the cause, since Carman wound up in surgery.

What have you tried? What has and hasn't worked? Injections, applications, manipulations and vibrations may have given some temporary relief. But all of these have something in common with the rest. Dr. Richard Schuster explains: "Experience has shown that in most cases rest is of little value since identical injuries soon occur as the patient starts running again."

Lasting relief comes with correcting the structural and functional shortcomings of the foot, and modifying its working environment. A runner can take care of the obvious changes himself.

PATTERNS OF WEAR

by Harry Hlavac D.P.M.

Dr. Hlavac, a distance runner, is a practicing podiatrist and an assistant professor at the California College of Podiatric Medicine.

Shoe wear patterns and the location of calluses on the feet indicate areas of stress during walking and running. While shoes wear down in areas of friction and stress, the body attempts to protect the deeper structures by *adding* protective layers of skin. Each tissue of the body reacts to stress in different ways, but all tissues follow the same stress syndrome. That is, in the reaction to stress there is a period of irritability, then a period of resistance, and finally a period of breakdown, or exhaustion.

Influence of Angle of Gait on Stress Lines

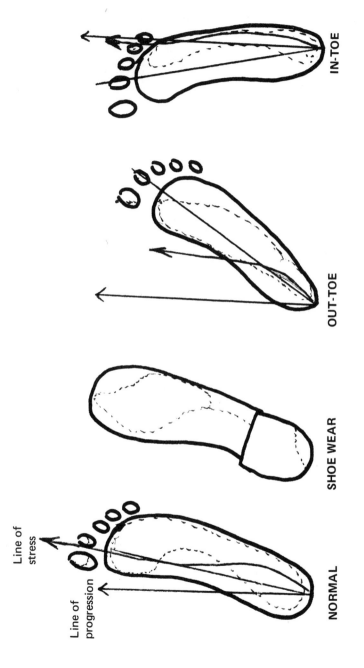

Line of stress

Line of progression

NORMAL

SHOE WEAR

OUT-TOE

IN-TOE

Not all abnormal shoe wear patterns are significant. They may indicate a structural imbalance problem, or they may reflect that the body has adequately compensated for a structural problem. However, specific calluses on the sole of the foot always indicate a progressive disorder which requires treatment.

The main purpose of the skin is the protection of the deeper structures from trauma. Under long-term stress, the top layer of the skin becomes inflamed and thickens. The thick skin puts pressure on the deeper structures, causing increasing pain and disability. Pressure over a broad area produces a large, diffuse callus. But over a specific metatarsal or bone spur, it may produce a deep,

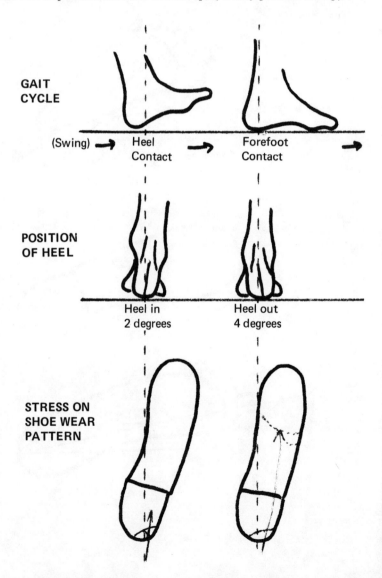

GAIT CYCLE

(Swing) → Heel Contact → Forefoot Contact →

POSITION OF HEEL

Heel in 2 degrees   Heel out 4 degrees

STRESS ON SHOE WEAR PATTERN

nucleated corn, putting pressure on nerves and vessels with progressively deeper problems.

Imbalance of the foot causes bone prominences. Compensation for foot imbalance causes friction and shearing stress between the bone, skin and the shoe. Soft padded shoes and socks minimize friction, but are not stable enough for active propulsion while running. A balance of protection, cushioning, flexibility at heel contact, and rigidity in propulsion is necessary for an efficient running style.

In running, the normal angle of gait (angle between the direction of the

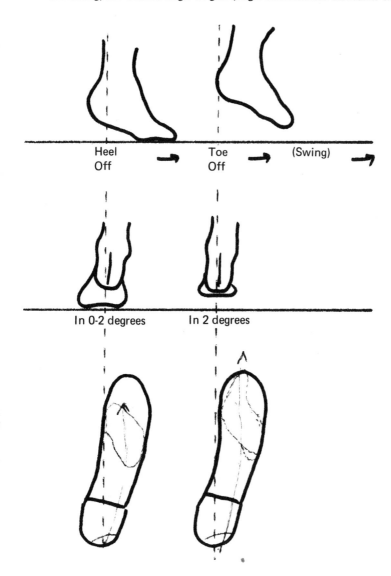

Heel Off   Toe Off   (Swing)

In 0-2 degrees   In 2 degrees

foot and the line of progression) is about 10 degrees, a mild out-toe. If the angle is greater than 10 degrees, the foot is inefficient because weight stress rides through the inside of the foot during propulsion. This produces lateral (outside) heel wear on the shoe and medial (inside) forefoot wear. An angle of gait of 0-10 degrees (straight ahead) is most efficient for propulsion. An angle less than 0 degrees (in-toed or "pigeon-toed") is inefficient because stress comes through the shorter lateral toes, and is also quite unstable. In-toed gait produces inner heel wear and outer forefoot wear of the shoe.

Stress lines through the foot are influenced by the angle of gait (see page 25). Angle of gait problems do not produce specific calluses because there are no shearing forces. However, they do produce "pinch" calluses around the borders of the foot, where the upper meets the sole of the shoe. Pinch calluses may also form where there are imbalance problems or because of improper shoe fit. Specific, more serious calluses develop from deeper mechanical problems.

In running, the foot serves two purposes. At heel contact, it is a "mobile adapter" for balance and to adapt to an uneven terrain. In propulsion, it is a "rigid lever" to push body weight forward. In order to become mobile, the foot pronates (a complex motion where the heel bone tilts out and the leg internally rotates). In order to became rigid, it supinates (motion at the same joint where the heel bone tilts in and the leg externally rotates).

Normally, at heel contact the heel bone is tilted 0-2 degrees inward, accounting for slight lateral heel wear on the shoe. It then rolls to the point where the forefoot comes down flat on the ground and the heel bone is tilted about four degrees outward. At this point, the stress is falling from the contact point of the heel of the shoe to the entire ball of the foot. As the leg comes over the foot, the heel bone tilts in again, making the foot rigid and ready for propulsion through the first and second toes (see page 27). Calluses form and shoes wear improperly when the foot is out of balance as it goes through these phases of the gait cycle.

Most imbalance problems are the result of inherited foot types. If you have calluses that are not yet painful, treatment may include cushioning of the irritated area with things like foam pads or Spenco insoles (available in pharmacies and most sporting good shops). Avoid all chemical "corn cure" medicines which are acids that burn normal skin as well as the corns and calluses. Severe burns can result.

Pain at specific pressure points on the soles of the feet can usually be temporarily relieved with felt padding applied directly on the foot, around or behind (never in front of) the friction areas. Cover the padding with a thin tape to prevent the edges from rolling. This padding will be adequate through a few miles and a couple of showers, but should be replaced daily. If this works well, then you can transfer this same padding into the shoe, where it will work for a longer duration. Permanent custom-made appliances can be fitted by a podiatrist. These work as protective padding, and to prevent calluses by correcting mechanical problems. Attempt commonsense remedies, but when necessary seek professional help.

INJURY FIRST AID

Injured athletes have a lot in common with wounded soldiers. A military hospital's purpose is to patch up soldiers and march them back to the lines to be shot at again. Much of sports medicine concentrates on killing pain so the athletes can run out and risk getting hurt again.

Immediate treatment of injuries is necessary, of course. But it's only first aid. It gives only temporary relief unless it's followed by preventive medicine. The aim in first aid should only be to get rid of the worst symptoms quickly so the real treatment can begin.

We'll get to preventive gimmicks later. But you can't do anything until you're feeling better, so you need first aid. Here's a quick review of the principles, most of which are familiar to runners:

● **Symptoms**—Stiffness, swelling, redness, heat, limping. If you have any combination of these, treat them now. Don't wait. They could get worse.

● **Rest**—It's a dirty word among addicted runners. But occasionally it's the only solution. If you can't run a step without limping dramatically, don't run. You'll aggravate the injury, and possibly produce another one somewhere else.

British sports physiotherapist Denis Wright advises, "By judicious treatment, nature can be assisted (in healing) and the processes speeded up slightly. Similarly, nature can be impeded and the healing processes delayed by interference. Unfortunately, athletes generally fail to recognize the most important aspect of treatment, which without doubt is that of rest."

Wright says the advice "run it off" and "go through the pain barrier" are "phrases of folly and ignorance."

● **Substitutes**—Bicycling appears to be the best one for sore-legged runners. It simulates the running action without many of its stresses.

Keith Hartman, an often-hurt distance man and competitive cyclist, says, "I have yet to find an injury that precludes bike riding, at least in low gear." He tells of hurting his arch. "After four months of exclusively bicycling, I began running again. I jogged an easy mile the first and second days, and on the third day ran a 4:58 mile (my best time has only been 4:30). Even more important, within four weeks of starting to run, I was racing better than ever in events from five miles up. My condition actually improved while riding the bike."

● **Reduced Running**—Let your pain threshold guide you. Run if pain doesn't restrict normal movement. But run only so long as pain remains constant or diminishes as you go. If it grows, stop! No fast running. No sudden changes of pace. No hills.

Dr. Paul Kiell adds, "Start with frequent, short runs, emphasizing proper form. No long runs for awhile." Try interval jogging-walking at first. Increase the running as pain levels allow.

● **Cold Water**—From Dr. George Sheehan's *Encyclopedia of Athletic Medicine*: "The first 48 hours after an injury occurs is considered the crucial period. Immediate and repeated cold applications reduce inflammation, which in turn slows swelling. Heat, in any form, during the first two-day period should be avoided since it has the opposite, undesirable effect."

The easiest way to apply cold is to fill a sock with ice cubes and wrap it around the injured area. Some doctors say, "Soak it in hot water after the first two days." But Dr. Sheehan notes, "Success has been reported recently with the continuous application of cold until the pain has vanished—or at least alternating cold and hot treatment. The reason continued cold may be beneficial, even after the first two days, is this: the runner is one of the few patients who reinjures himself daily. Each workout may cause damage, though so slight it's almost unnoticed. Applying cold after each workout may keep this damage in check while healing progresses."

Remember, though, that these are first aid steps. They promise no more than to put you back on your feet, back to the "front line" where the injury happened.

CHOOSING SHOES

by Joe Henderson

My only qualification for being here as a layman in a pack of doctors is that I've suffered a lot. I'm a running medical dictionary: achilles tendinitis, bursitis, calf muscle tear...and most of the rest of the way through the alphabet.

I'm not writing because I'm unique, but because I'm so disgustingly normal among long-time runners. Any runner who has been at it for 10 or 20 years can tell the same story, which mixes frustration with a strange kind of "look-how-I've-overcome-the-pain" pride.

Jim Dare, an interantionalist in the steeplechase (an event containing more than the usual number of painful incidents) and Ritchie Geisel (a runner with a longer medical record than mine) have outlined what they call the "constant pain level theory."

Dare and Geisel say every runner carries X amount of pain around with him all the time. It's something to talk about, to complain about. The pain is migratory. Sometimes it's in the stomach, sometimes in the foot, sometimes somewhere in between. It may be a dull ache spread throughout the body, or it may be a sharp one concentrated in a spot no bigger than a thumb print. But it's always there. If it isn't really there, runners imagine it is.

But as Dr. Steve Subotnick told me a couple of years ago, the pains don't count as more than conversation pieces until runners can't run on them any more. Only then do we go to the doctor. I visited Dr. Subotnick after I'd broken myself down to a hobble. He told me what was wrong and got me to running again. He said I was a one-man disaster area: tibial varum, cavus arch, equinus foot, rectocalcaneal exostoses of the heels, and a bunch of other words I didn't understand.

He put plastic inserts in my shoes—"golden arches," they came to be called—and cut a hunk of bony growth out of one heel, and did a lot of other things that cost too much time and money. In my case, they had to be done, and I'm happy I found the podiatrist when I did. But if I hadn't made some incredibly dumb moves in all the years before, I might have never needed any of this.

SOME ASSUMPTIONS

That's all they are—assumptions drawn from my own trials and errors, and the ones I see other runners making all the time.

1. The feet and legs can accept a tremendous amount of abuse. Knowing what I now do about the "deformities" most runners have, I'm not surprised at how often we get hurt. I'm surprised we're as healthy as we are. My foot architecture is disastrous, the podiatrist says. Yet in 15 or 16 years of running before I learned of these problems and of corrective measures, all but two years were relatively pain-free. By using nothing more exotic than exercise and restraint, we can stop most injuries before they happen.

2. Overworking hurts the worst. Runners break down when they do too much training, too much racing or both. I've never had the mileage required to run a marathon without "collapsing" somewhere near the end. No one, in my estimation, is up to racing more than 5-10% of his miles. I've run more than two dozen marathons, and shortly before visiting Dr. Subotnick had some 20%, 30% and even 40% racing months. (See the booklet *Run Gently Run Long* for more on this subject.)

3. Runners tighten up. And tight muscles and their connections get hurt. They're like guitar strings that have gone past proper tuning and will snap with slight extra twists. Stretching exercises relieve much of the tension. Up to the time I went into surgery, I had never done any stretching. I couldn't pick up a pencil from the floor without getting down on my hands and knees. (Exercises are described in detail in *Exercises for Runners.*)

4. The best exercise for feet is barefoot walking and running. The healthiest feet are those which go naked over soft surfaces. Dr. William Rossi wrote 20 years ago in *Your Feet and Their Care*, "Most foot troubles are caused, directly or indirectly, by shoes. Perhaps nothing can illustrate this more graphically than a foot survey that was made in India and China among the natives who habitually go bareofot. Whereas in the United States similar studies reveal that about 85% of the adult population is foot-defective, the India-China study in which 5000 natives were examined showed an incidence of foot defects of only 7%."

My feet felt their best when I could still run barefoot on grass. I can't do that very often any more. The available surfaces are in even worse shape than my feet.

5. Shoes cause as much trouble as they prevent. That's a fair assumption to draw from Dr. Rossi's research. Shoes rub the feet the wrong way, causing blisters, calluses, corns, bunions, bursitis, etc. They lift the heels and disturb normal posture. They lock the feet in a semi-rigid cast and prevent them from exercising fully.

Since we've always worn shoes, we probably have to keep wearing them—realizing that shoddy shoes complicate existing problems and the best shoes may only hold the line against further damage.

For seven years, I wore shoes that rate among the worst in the features podiatrists consider important. They were badly made, badly fitted and—after the first month or two—badly worn. This, on top of overwork and inflexibility was a final insult the "deformed" legs and feet wouldn't tolerate.

THE SHOES YOU CHOOSE

There is no "perfect shoe." Discounting for now the matters of individual needs and preferences, there still is no running shoe without at least one significant defect. Most shoes have several flaws big enough to cause or aggravate an injury.

Podiatrists have given me leads on what features to look for in running shoes. Style and price aren't among them. Where the health of the feet and legs are concerned, forget fashion and bend your budget for the sake of safety, support, durability and comfort.

I spent several days looking over the most popular training shoes (specialized shoes such as spikes and "waffles" weren't included), and grading them A-B-C in eight important areas. The ratings are rather arbitrary, but they help show where shoes are strongest and weakest.

1. Sole Wear and Cushion. Obviously, shoes that wear out quickest get run over at the heels first. A worn spot as small as a quarter-inch can create a destructive imbalance at foot contact. The most durable shoes have a hard outer sole with a softer cushioning layer underneath. This layer is primarily designed to absorb shock.

A—two-layer sole, each at least one-fourth inch at toe and heel.
B—two-layer sole, one less than one-fourth inch.
C—single-layer sole under all or part of the foot.

2. Sole Flexibility. The forefoot flexes dramatically at toe-off. So, too, must the shoe. If the shoe doesn't bend easily, the stress is taken up by the front and back of the leg. Stiff shoes are suspected of causing some types of achilles tendon and shin problems.

A—shoe bend (at ball of foot) to 90-degree angle by pressing the fingers against the front.

B—can be bent to 90 degrees by holding front and back of the shoe and flexing wrists.

C—need full-arm force to bend the shoe to 90 degrees.

3. Shank Support. Podiatrists point to the cutaway shank, the area under the arch, as the suspected source of many heel and arch complaints. When a runner hits the ground with several hundred pounds of force per square inch, the "bridge" buckles, throwing a strain onto the foot. The shoe sole at the arch should be flush with the ground.

A—solid, rigid shank.

B—partial "bridge" under arch.

C—full "bridge."

4. Heel Lift. Ideally, the running shoe heel is higher than the street shoe heel. The achilles tendon and calves are accustomed to support in walking, and need it all the more in running. Measurements of heel lift are taken by subtracting the thickness of the sole under the big toe from the maximum thickness of the heel.

A—one-half inch or more.

B—three-eighths inch.

C—one-fourth inch or less.

5. Interior Support. Arch supports are like eye glasses. If you need them, then you need individually prescribed ones. The arch sponges added by most shoe manufacturers don't do much good because they're all alike and they're too soft to do much supporting. Harder, built-in arch and heel counters are a little better.

A—built-in arch support and/or heel cup.

B—removable sponge rubber arch cushion.

C—no arch support.

6. Upper Softness. Leathers, even the fancy suedes that start glove-soft, get hard from the weather and from age. Brittle leather causes blisters. Nylon stays softest for the life of the shoe.

A—nylon upper.

B—suede (reversed) leather.

C—standard leather.

7. Heel Counter. This is the hard piece at the back of the shoe, designed to stabilize the heel. This heel control is essential to anyone who has been hurt, and the importance of the counter grows with heel height.

A—rigid counter covering entire heel area.

B—semi-rigid counter covering entire heel area.

C—minimal or no counter (back of shoe easily flattened with fingers).

8. Weight. Most racing shoes are well below 10 ounces apiece. Medium-weight all-purpose shoes weigh 10-12 ounces, and the heavy-duty models are above 12 ounces. The ratings here are based on size nine shoes.

A—under 10 ounces per shoe.

B—10-11 ounces.

C—12 ounces or more.

Surveying the Running Shoe Market

Shoe Brand and Model	Sole Makeup	Sole Bend	Shank Support	Heel Lift	Inside Support	Upper Softness	Heel Counter	Shoe Weight
Adidas Country	B	B	A	B	B	C	B	B
Adidas Dragon	C	A	A	B	B	A	A	A
Adidas Gazelle	B	A	A	A	B	B	A	B
Adidas Italia	B	A	A	B	B	C	A	B
Adidas Marathon	B	A	B	C	A	B	B	A
Adidas Olympia	B	A	A	B	B	C	A	C
Adidas Rom	C	B	A	B	B	C	A	B
Adidas SL-72	B	A	A	A	B	A	A	B
Brooks Drake	A	B	A	B	B	A	A	A
Brooks Texas	C	A	A	C	B	A	A	A
E.B. Lydiard R.R.	A	B	A	B	A	B	B	B
E.B. Marathon	C	A	B	A	A	B	B	A
New Balance Speedster	B	A	A	B	B	A	C	A
New Balance Trackster III	B	A	A	B	B	B	B	C
Nike Boston 73	B	A	A	C	A	A	C	A
Nike Cortez (Deluxe)	A	B	A	B	B	B	A	C
Nike Cortez (Leather)	A	B	A	B	B	C	C	C
Nike Cortez (Nylon)	A	B	A	B	B	A	C	C

	1	2	3	4	5	6	7	8
Nike Finland/Kenya	A	B	A	B	B	A	C	A
Nike Marathon	B	A	C	C	C	A	C	A
Puma Crack	B	A	A	B	B	B	A	C
Puma 9190	B	A	A	B	B	A	A	B
Tiger Boston	B	A	A	B	B	A	C	A
Tiger Cortez	A	B	A	B	B	C	B	C
Tiger Jayhawk	B	A	A	B	B	A	A	A
Tiger Marathon	B	A	C	C	C	A	C	A
Tiger Montreal	A	B	A	B	B	A	A	B
Tiger Munich	A	C	A	B	B	C	B	C
Tiger Tahoe	B	B	A	C	B	B	C	C
Tiger Vickka	B	B	A	B	B	C	B	C

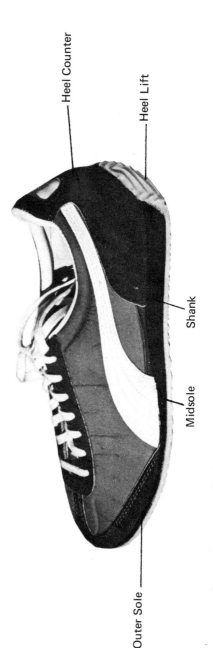

Heel Counter

Heel Lift

Shank

Midsole

Outer Sole

The chart (pages 34-35) summarizes the features of 30 models worn most frequently by runners. All these checks were made from new, size nine shoes. No attempt is made to rate the shoes 1-30 since people's needs vary so much. One person might need a rigid heel counter, for instance, while another gets along nicely with a flimsy-backed shoe. The gradings are to indicate to people who have trouble in specific areas which shoes are considered best in these areas. B and C ratings don't imply that shoes are defective in any way, only that they rank slightly below other models.

GIVING RUNNERS FITS

"I have repeatedly noticed chronic injuries occurring in runners who wear shoes that are either too narrow or too wide," writes Dr. Gabe Mirkin in *The Complete Runner*. He's disgusted with shoemakers who ignore this detail, which means he's disgusted with almost all of them.

He says, "Instead of having widths, they prefer to confuse the runner with hundreds of different shoes which vary only slightly... New Balance is the only company making a serious effort to help the runner who doesn't have average feet. Most other brands come in a standard C or D width."

And what if you don't have C or D feet but don't want New Balance shoes? If the feet are narrower, Dr. Mirkin recommends adding a Spenco insole to the shoes. But this only cuts the width down by one letter (D to C, for instance). If your feet are slimmer than that, you have a problem no Adidas, Nike, Puma, Tiger, etc., can solve. A shoe that is snug enough will cramp the toes into the front end. One that is long enough will leave the feet to wander from side to side in the shoe.

Wide-footed people have more of a problem since most running shoes come to a point in front. Tracings of their feet don't come close to matching the shape of the shoes. The toes are crammed into a shoe which is the right length. (Mirkin says the longest toe should be about three-fourths of an inch from the end of the shoe.) To relieve cramping, they have to buy a shoe that is a half-size or more too long.

Both narrow feet and too-big shoes lead to complications at the heel. The shoe fits loosely, the heel "wanders." This is doubly true in shoes without adequate heel counters.

"You can correct this problem," Dr. Mirkin writes, "by putting moleskin on the sides of the shoe's heel and covering the moleskin with rubber tape. Be careful not to run the moleskin around the back of the shoe, as it will shorten it and push the foot too far forward." (See page 39.)

CARE AND REPAIR

The pattern was so familiar, I wonder why I was so slow to identify the cause and effect. Two or three months into a new pair of Tiger Bostons, I'd break through the hard outer layer of heel and go into the softer midsole. About the same time, I'd start to get pains in my achilles tendons and calves. They'd get worse quickly as the wear accelerated. Then I'd buy new shoes. Within a couple of weeks, the pains would go away—only to return as heel wear again passed a critical point. My critical point was about a quarter-inch.

I should mention here that I'm a klutz who can't spread butter without missing the bread. I'd heard, as I once wrote in *Runner's World*, of "all the goops and patches and replacement parts" for heels. All required talents I didn't have and refused to learn. So I let my heels wear away as God intended.

Then the electric glue gun entered my life. I can't say it's the best way to fix shoes. But it certainly is the easiest. Plug the gun's cord into a wall socket. Melt the glue bullet for 10 minutes. Squirt a few drops of glue onto the wear area. Smooth and thin it with the hot barrel. The shoes are ready for running as soon as the glue cools and hardens. With luck, the glue will last a week before it wears away and needs replacing.

I use glue only to protect newish shoes. Trying to resurrect old, badly worn ones is more trouble than it's worth. And I use only paper-thin layers of glue. A quarter-inch raised glob can cause as much damage as a quarter-inch of wear.

The worst damage I've done with the gun is to burn my fingers trying to spread the molten glue. It's the worst running-related injury I've had for some time now.

SELF - SUPPORTING

Tom Knatt is a man of diverse talents. He works as a guitar maker in West Concord, Mass., places well in local road runs, and race walks fast enough to compete in the Olympic Trials. And he writes. An article of his is in *The Complete Runner*.

Knatt tells there how he hurt his achilles tendon while race walking. It bothered him for most of a year, and he followed the usual symptomatic remedies without luck. Then he injured the arch of the other foot.

"Feeling very discouraged," he writes, "I mentioned the arch problem to a woman at the New Balance Athletic Shoe Company. She suggested I try her 'cookies.' These are arch supports, made of semi-hard sponge rubber and shaped like a flying saucer with one edge cut off. (The square edge fits against the side of the shoe. The rounded part supports the arch itself.)"

Tom bought the cookies, "wearing one in my left shoe only to help that arch. That trouble cleared up shortly, but I kept wearing the support. I added one in the other shoe, only to keep a feeling of symmetry. To my great surprise and pleasure, the achilles tendon pain cleared up in about a week."

A few weeks later, Knatt ran 2:39—his best time—in the Boston marathon. "I had no problems with the tendon, during or after the race," he says.

We've dropped hints several places already in this booklet of how simple, homemade supports and shoe modifications can reverse the course of injuries. The previous article and the earlier one in this chapter by Dr. Harry Hlavac discuss various types of padding.

"Most runners," says Dr. George Sheehan, "need some support in their shoes." Most foot doctors agree that the soft sponge arch supports in running shoes are inadequate. They agree that something more substantial should replace them. They only disagree on the specifics.

Dr. Sheehan says, 'I sometimes make the analogy to eye problems. If you have a minor reading problem, you can do quite well with a pair of glasses you buy at Woolworth's. If your foot problem is minor, and you're lucky, you can get by with a store-bought arch and a heel lift.''

Sheehan thinks Dr. Scholl's supports might be enough for mild problems. The types he recommends are Flexo, 610 and Athletic A.

Dr. Gabe Mirkin agrees in principle, but not in method. He discourages runners from using Dr. Scholl's inserts because "they raise the heel of the foot out of the shoe. This gives less stability."

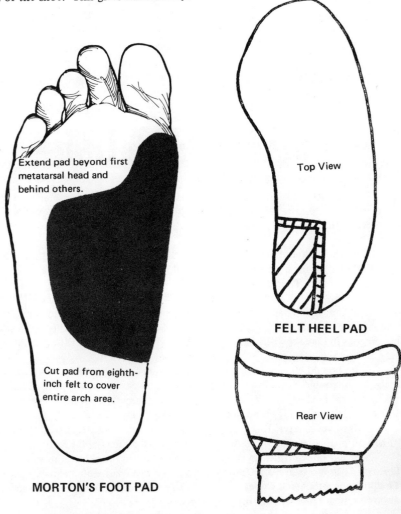

Extend pad beyond first metatarsal head and behind others.

Cut pad from eighth-inch felt to cover entire arch area.

MORTON'S FOOT PAD

Top View

FELT HEEL PAD

Rear View

Mirkin sides with Tom Knatt in favoring the arch "cookie." (Available from some shoe repair shops or from the New Balance Athletic Shoe Company, 176 Belmont, Watertown, Mass. 02172.) These supports reduce the pronation of the foot, which is said to cause a number of foot-leg injuries.

"As everyone's arch is different," Dr. Mirkin notes, "it will take some manipulation to fit the cookie to your foot. Do not glue in the cookie until you have found your fit. The cookies are best kept in place with two-sided adhesive tape. If the cookies feel too high, they can be filed down."

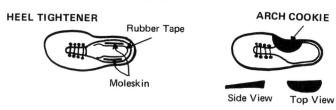

HEEL TIGHTENER   Rubber Tape   **ARCH COOKIE**

Moleskin   Side View   Top View

Dr. Steve Subotnick, a podiatrist, is more cautious in the area of self-treatment than are the two M.D.'s. He thinks the only absolutely effective support is an "orthotic" molded to the shape of one's foot by a professional. (More on this in Chapter Three.)

However, Subotnick does concede that properly made do-it-yourself supports are better than none at all. He teaches his runner-patients how to make theirs from felt.

"At times," he says, "the use of felt inside of a well-constructed running shoe will correct minimal imbalances and those symptoms associated with them will lessen. At other times, the pain will be decreased but still bothersome. Failure of felt does not mean that a well-made orthotic fashioned from a neutral cast of your foot will fail. The difference in control available with felt and more rigid material is considerable."

MAKING FELT INSERTS, by Steven Subotnick D.P.M.

The material can be purchased from a pharmacy or surgical supply house. If you have difficulty in obtaining it, call your local podiatrist. He will be able to provide it, or tell you where you can get it. Felt with adhesive on one side is easiest to use. If this isn't available, use two-sided tape to hold the material inside the shoe.

- **Quarter-Inch Heel Pads.** Since most runners have some bowing of the lower one-third of their legs, we have found that quarter-inch felt pads on the *inside* (behind the hollow of the arch) of the heel is helpful for controlling minor malpositions. The felt is highest on the inside edge, and is cut so it tapers down and there is no felt beyond the middle of the heel. (See page 38.)

A bow-legged (varus) condition causes runner's knee, shin splints, heel bumps and other injuries. Placing the felt pad on the inside of your heel helps reduce the abnormal turning in of the ankle which occurs at foot plant.

- **Quarter-Inch Arch Pads.** A half-heart shaped felt pad is cut to the shape of the arch, again being highest on the inside (where the arch is highest) and tapered. This pad may help lessen symptoms associated with foot strain, muscle pulls, shin splints and knee problems which appear to be related to a sagging arch. The arch pad may be placed in the shoe or taped to the foot.

- **Eighth-Inch Surgical Felt.** This may be utilized for additional padding under the heel bone for heel spurs, bone bruises or bursitis. The area which is painful should be accommodated. Cut the felt away from that area and build up a border around it, providing a "valley" for the tender spot. Build up the opposite heel by the same amount so that no low-back pain results from an imbalance.

A "Morton's Foot" (short first metatarsal or hypermobile first metatarsal) will benefit from an eighth-inch buildup under the first metatarsal. This adds stability to the arch of the foot. (See page 38.)

EXERCISES FOR FEET
by Charles A. Palmer

Charles Palmer, of Portland, Ore., a competitive weight lifter-turned-runner, contributed the weight training section to the booklet Exercises for Runners.

Foot exercises? What is a *foot* exercise? Competitive runners know that fast intervals and racing are good exercises for speed. Sprinters can find any number of leg and arm exercises to help develop an explosive start. Runners seeking to build endurance can easily fashion a program using intervals and steady distance to meet their individual needs. But most runners wouldn't recognize a foot exercise if one came riding by on an arch support.

I can almost hear runners saying, "Foot exercises? Who needs foot exercises? I give them enough exercise running 10 miles a day."

Well, maybe. But runners could profit from other forms of foot exercise. I base this assumption on a quick glance at the injury list in the booklet *Shoes for Runners*, taken from a poll of 1600-plus active runners. More than 48% of the injuries listed are of the foot itself (if we count the achilles tendon and ankle as parts of the foot). This does not take into account the fact that a fair percentage of the rest of the injuries (especially those of the knee, shin, hip and back) are directly linked to prbblems beginning at the foot. It would seem that building strength and flexibility into the foot with specific exercises could do a lot to improve this sad situation.

If there are villains in this scenario, they are the hard surfaces we normally walk and run on, and the shoes that our feet are encased in during our waking hours. The hard surfaces concentrate stress unnaturally in the foot, while shoes limit the freedom of the feet to absorb these shocks. The stresses built up in running are at least quadruple those of walking because of landing from a greater height and at more than doubled speed.

I began to run after spending a few years in the sport of competitive Olympic weight lifting, during which time I experienced no injury that came close to interrupting my schedule of training on alternate days. Even the dreaded deep knee-bend caused nothing more serious than minor discomfort when negotiating stairs on the day following a heavy workout. From the start, my experience with running injuries was not nearly as mundane.

During a break-in period of several months before I reached a seven-mile run, I was plagued with knee, ankle and heel problems. When the heel problem didn't respond to rest, simple arch supports or a cortisone shot, I began to think the solution to all my aches and pains (and those of all other runners) must lie in custom orthotic devices. But before I raised the money to buy a pair, which may or may not have been needed, I began to explore the idea of injury prevention through simple exercises which could promote strength and flexibility in the runner's basic platform: the foot.

FOOT EXERCISES

Maximum effect is generally obtained if each exercise is performed barefoot.

1. Calf Raise(strengthens the arch and stretches the achilles tendon): On an elevated surface such as a stairstep or thick book, position feet so that the toes alone support the feet. If this is too difficult at first, start on the balls of the feet and move back gradually. Rise up on toes as far as possible. Sink as low as possible and pause for seven seconds in the bottom position. Do the movement slowly and without jerks or bounces. Weights may be added for more resistance, or one can alternate between single feet. Work up to 20 or more repetitions.

2. Walk Variations (preferably on a carpet, soft ground or grass): Walk around on the outer edges of the feet...on the inner edges of the feet...on the heels...on tiptoes. Try for a minute each way.

3. Soft Drink Bottle Exercise (for flexibility and circulation; do on a carpet): Seated—Roll the bottle with firm pressure from heel to toe, using both feet. Standing—Use more pressure and alternate feet. Do each for one minute. (A Coke bottle works well because of the convex-concave variation in shape. Split the time between the two curves.)

4. Marble Pick-up: From a seated position, pick up a marble or other small, round object. Practice pick-up with each toe for a total of two minutes per foot.

5. Pencil Exercise: Put a pencil below the toes, pointing outward, and grasp by curling the toes. Try to write your name, which you will be able to do as you get stronger. Do the same with the pencil placed vertically between two toes. (Alternate between different toes.) More muscles come into play as you become more dextrous.

6. Toe Grip on Book: Put your toes over the edge of a thick book (opposite the binding), and grip the cover. Apply grip intermittently during a total period of one minute per foot, increasing the force of the grip each day. The toe grip can be developed to a degree surpassing the strength of the fingers. A friend of mine could lift a metal trash can with ease using his toes.

3

Podiatrists

Dr. George Sheehan is 30 years into his medical career, specializing in cardiology. He can't change directions now. But he says if he had it to do over again, he'd concentrate on the feet instead of the heart. The feet are where the exciting new steps in sports medicine are being taken.

"There is no question," he recently told a prospective medical student, "that given one choice I would pick podiatry." Podiatrists, Sheehan says, are coming the closest to treating the causes of athletic injuries, which in most cases begin in the feet.

The doctor has written, "While the doctors of podiatric medicine wait in the wings to apply these remedies, sports medicine continues to provide unimaginative, inadequate and ineffectual care of the ailing runner. At the present time, the medical profession's batting average against runners' occupational hazards is close to zero. When the cause is unknown, prevention is unknown. Treatment comes down to an attack on symptoms and not the cause."

An example is the use of drugs—cortisone, butazolidine, indocin—for tendon injuries. Dr. Gabe Mirkin, another M.D. runner who's disenchanted with his colleagues, says, "Cortisone injections only take down the swelling for a few days and never correct the problem. Two or three injections into the same tendon can result in the tendon pulling away from the bone or muscle. Butazolidine and indocin take down the inflammation only as long as you take the drugs. As soon as you stop, the pain returns."

Some podiatrists, too, have picked up the drug habit from other branches of medicine. But their therapy usually centers on correcting foot-plant problems. Their main tool is the orthotic, a custom-made support which fits into shoes. Theoretically, the orthotics control the stresses which produce injuries.

But before you run out to have yourself fitted for these devices, you should know this about podiatrists. First, there aren't many podiatrists, and second, few of them appreciate the needs of athletes.

Dr. Sheehan says, "We only graduate 300 podiatrists a year—six a state. When we take those interested in our (runners') problems, it goes down even more. And very few of these are yet accepted as part of the sports medicine

team. We need a specialist, but not many are available. This won't come until podiatry reaches the point of acceptance that all other specialties have."

That point apparently won't be reached soon. Dr. Sheehan reports that a
poll of physicians ranked podiatrists 41st in importance out of 42 health science
professions—just below licensed practical nurses. This despite the fact that podiatrists have four years of professional training beyond their undergraduate work,
and many are licensed to perform surgery.

Physicians continue to carry the major burden of athletic treatment. With
rare exceptions, they prescribe injections, pills, taping and rest. The results, at
best, are spotty. An eastern sports podiatrist who puts orthotics under runners
can say that in four years "we haven't had a complete failure."

BEST FOOT FORWARD

If all else fails, visit a podiatrist who's a runner or who knows enough about
athletics to offer more than "take six weeks off" advice. When rest, exercises
and self-help methods have failed, a podiatrist may have the kind of support you
need.

They call their devices orthotics, inserts, appliances, arch supports. These
are made different ways, of different materials ranging from leather to cork to
plastic. But the basic idea behind them is the same: to normalize abnormal feet.
If the feet don't meet the ground as they should, podiatrists construct platforms
to correct the situation.

The orthotics have proven to be effective for a majority of runners who
use them. But you should know their disadvantages, too. They're expensive—
generally $100 or more. The break-in period with some types is rather long and
painful. They usually require bigger shoes than you're now wearing, and can't
be worn at all in some models. And they cut down somewhat on freedom of
movement, particularly at high speeds.

But if they correct severe and chronic problems, the orthotics are worth the
bother. Here, Dr. Steve Subotnick, executive secretary of the American Academy of Podiatric Sports Medicine, answers questions on orthotics. While he pre-
fers to use the plastic type, other podiatrists may use softer and more flexible materials.

What are the purposes of orthotics?

This type of appliance offers functional control. The orthotics control heel
contact, midstance and toe-off. They do not weaken the foot but actually make
it stronger by allowing the muscles and tendons to function around a stable bony
architecture. The orthotics have been shown to reduce overuse syndromes of the
feet, ankles, lower legs, knees, thighs, hips and back.

How are these appliances made?

The orthotics are made from a positive cast of the patient's foot. The positive cast comes from a negative cast of the foot as it is held in a non-weight-bearing, "neutral" position. This is the position that allows for the most efficient as well as the safest functioning of the foot.

We then make our orthotics from a thermal-liable plastic with limited flexibility. Depending on the patient's needs, we may apply "posts" to the front or rear of the orthotic to control forefoot or heel function. Shock-absorbing material may be placed over the (plastic) surface of the orthotic.

What type of athlete can use the rigid orthotics?

The rigid orthotics are designed to be used in street shoes for everyday use, and in training or competition shoes for long distance work. The orthotics are for distance running and walking. They are not for field events or for competition below the mile.

In reality, we're more concerned with speed than distance. Some runners are up on their toes at five-minute mile pace and some at six-minute mile pace. The point is, many runners need a more flexible, softer orthotic for faster speeds, competition and for runs over very rough terrain. Almost all field events call for a more flexible support. The rigid support is designed for the heel-foot-toe or foot-toe type of gait found in slower distance activity.

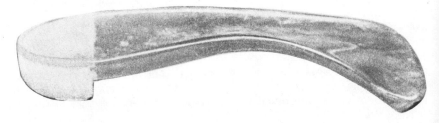

Side view of a plastic orthotic fitted with a rearfoot post.

I find it advantageous for almost all of my patients to have both pairs of orthotics. The soft orthotic is dispensed first and helps get the patient ready for the more rigid type, as well as being used in instances where the rigid appliance is undesirable.

Can all athletes tolerate rigid orthotics?

The orthotics are well-tolerated by about 85% of my patients during actual running. They are well-tolerated by 98% of my patients during normal walking. Non-tolerance is due primarily to blister formation as well as the fact that some runners dislike the added weight of the foot support.

All plastic orthotics need adjustment from time to time. One of the major problems in breaking in these appliances is the blistering which may occur on the longitudinal arch. This can be lessened by minor lowering of the arch and by placing materials such as Spenco over the plastic after final adjustments have been made.

Patients who refuse to go through the break-in period are in effect robbing themselves and the doctor of a probably favorable result.

What does this break-in period involve?

Although the athlete can readily wear the orthotics in his street shoes with little difficulty, it takes from 4-6 weeks to become fully accustomed to them in running shoes. I advise patients to begin by running only a mile or two a day in orthotics and to gradually increase the distance as they can do so without discomfort.

How effective are rigid orthotics compared to more flexible types of support?

Reviews of motion-analysis films of runners with various soft in-the-shoe pads demonstrates that very little abnormal pronation is being prevented or controlled.

Soft orthotics with rearfoot and forefoot posts made of rubber or felt have the advantage of being well-tolerated by runners, and they allow the runner to have a device which can be worn in street shoes and different pairs of running shoes, including spikes. However, films of runners with those devices show that excessive pronation is not prevented.

Review of films of runners wearing rigid orthotics shows that excellent control can be achieved. Angles of gait are changed and toe-off power is increased.

The control of symptoms in runners using the rigid appliances has been better than expected. Almost all of my running patients have been able to continue running with lessening to complete disappearance of foot-related overuse syndromes. Surgery has been required in some cases, following which orthotics appear to aid foot rehabilitation.

Do the orthotics become a "crutch" to the runner? Is he totally dependent on these devices once he begins using them?

I explain to runners that orthotics are not a crutch but allow the bony architecture of the foot to be in such a position that the muscles can function more efficiently and effectively. They do not cause atrophy of the foot which makes the foot totally dependent upon the orthotics.

REFERENCES

Sources are listed in the order that they appear in the booklet.

FOREWORD

Sheehan, George—"From the Ground Up," *Encyclopedia of Athletic Medicine*, Booklet No. 12, June 72, pp. 25-26.

"It All Starts Here," *Shoes for Runners*, Booklet No. 25, July 73, p. 67.

Henderson, Joe—"Steering Clear of Bumps," *Runner's World*, March 73, pp. 28-29

CHAPTER ONE

Sheehan, George—"Medical Advice," *Runner's World*, Sept. 71, p. 38.

Sheehan, George—"Look First at Feet," *Encyclopedia of Athletic Medicine*, Booklet No. 12, June 72, pp. 26-27.

Subotnick, Steven—"Shoes and Injuries," *Shoes for Runners*, Booklet No. 25, July 73, pp. 70-71.

Pagliano, John—"Foot Notes," *Track Technique*, No. 57, Sept. 74, pp. 1827-1828

Sheehan, George—"Morton's Foot: The Big Crippler?" *Runner's World*, Aug. 74, p. 23.

Mirkin, Gabe—"Get a Shoe That Fits," *The Complete Runner*, World Publication 1974, pp. 221-223.

Subotnick, Steven—"Long Legs, Short Legs," *Runner's World*, March 73, p. 21.

"It All Starts Here,"*Shoes for Runners*, Booklet No. 25, July 73, p. 67.

Schuster, Richard—"Causative Factors in Foot and Leg Problems in Runners," *New York RRC Newsletter*, Summer 74, p. 13.

Clancy, William—"Runner's Knee Symptoms," *Encyclopedia of Athletic Medicine*, Booklet No. 12, June 72, pp. 48-52.

Henderson, Joe—"The Runner's Final Stretch," *Runner's World*, Jan. 73, pp. 41-43.

Henderson, Joe—"The Legacy of Achilles," *Runner's World*, May 72, pp. 45-48.

Pagliano, John—"Achilles Aid," *Runner's World*, Sept. 72, pp. 38-39.

Subotnick, Steven—"Toe Trouble," *Runner's World*, April 74, p. 8.

"Shin Splint Causes," *Encyclopedia of Athletic Medicine*, Booklet No. 12, June 72, p. 43.

Ullyot, Joan—"Training Applications," *The Female Runner*, Booklet No. 34, April 74, pp. 20-22.

Subotnick, Steven—"Steering Clear of Bumps," *Runner's World*, March 73, pp. 28-30.

Sheehan, George and Subotnick, Steven—"Dealing with Sciatic Nerves," *Runner's World*, March 74, pp. 20-21.

CHAPTER TWO

Subotnick, Steven—"Long Legs, Short Legs," *Runner's World*, March 73, p. 21.

Carman, Bob—"Achilles Sufferer Finds Relief," *Guide to Distance Running,* World Publications, 1971, p. 25.

Wright, Denis—"The Curse of Achilles Pain," *Guide to Distance Running,* World Publications, 1971, pp. 22-24.

Hartman, Keith—"Pedaling to Health," *Runner's World,* Nov. 74, p. 24.

Kiell, Paul—"While an Injury is Mending," *Runner's World,* April 74, pp. 30-31.

Sheehan, George—"Treating with Water," *Encyclopedia of Athletic Medicine,* Booklet No. 12, June 72, p. 34.

Schuster, Richard—"Causative Factors of Foot and Leg Problems in Runners," *New York RRC Newsletter,* Summer 74, p. 13.

Mirkin, Gabe—"Get a Shoe That Fits," *The Complete Runner,* World Publications, 9174, pp. 221-223.

Subotnick, Steven—"Shoes and Injuries," *Shoes for Runners,* Booklet No. 25, July 73, pp. 70-71.

Henderson, Joe—*Run Gently, Run Long,* Booklet No. 29, p. 34.

Exercises for Runners, Booklet No. 29, Nov. 73.

Rossi, William—*Your Feet and Their Care,* Emerson Books Inc., New York, 1955.

Mirkin, Gabe—"House Call," *Starting Line Magazine,* March-April 74, pp. 18-19.

Henderson, Joe—"Happiness is a Warm Gun," *Runner's World,* Nov. 73, pp. 14-15.

Knatt, Tom—"Home Remedies," *The Complete Runner,* World Publications, 1974, pp. 212-216.

Walker, Morton—*Your Guide to Foot Health,* Arco Publishing, New York, 1972.

Bragg, Paul C.—*Building Strong Feet—Nature's Way,* Health Science, Burbank, Calif. 1973.

Hall, George J.—*Healthy Feet for All,* Health for All Publishing, Surrey, England, 1955.

CHAPTER THREE

Sheehan, George—"Loving Care for Feet," *Shoes for Runners,* Booklet No. 25, July 73, pp. 68-69.

Mirkin, Gabe—"Drugs Aren't the Answer," *Runner's World,* May 73, p. 19.

Henderson, Joe—"Adding Insert to Injury," *Runner's World,* July 73, pp. 16-17.